TROPICAL RAIN FORESTS

A TRUE BOOK

by

Darlene R. Stille

Children's Press®

A Division of Grolier Publishing

New York London Hong Kong Sydney
Danbury, Connecticut

Plants sometimes grow on the trunks of rain forest trees.

Reading Consultant
Linda Cornwell
*Coordinator of School Quality
and Professional Improvement
Indiana State Teachers
Association*

**Content Consultant
Jan Jenner, Ph.D.**

Author's Dedication
*For Cynthia A. Marquard,
who showed me some of the
world's great ecosystems*

*The photo on the cover
shows an area of Tapanti
National Park in Costa Rica.
The photo on the title page
shows rain forest trees
covered with moss.*

Library of Congress Cataloging-in-Publication Data

Stille, Darlene R.
    Tropical rain forests / by Darlene R. Stille.
        p.   cm. — (A True book)
    Includes bibliographical references and index.
    Summary: Differentiates a tropical rain forest from all others, and
describes its typical plant and animal life.
    ISBN: 0-516-21511-6 (lib.bdg.)   0-516-26774-4 (pbk.)
    1. Rain forests—Juvenile literature. 2. Rain forest ecology— Juvenile
literature. [1. Rain forests. 2. Rain forest ecology. 3. Ecology.] I. Title.
II. Series.
QH86.S74   1999
578.734—dc21   98-50753
                                                                      CIP
                                                                      AC

Contents

An evergreen rain forest in Washington

What Is a Rain Forest?

How are rain forests different from other forests? The answer is easy. They get more rain.

The rain forests that grow in cool places like the northwestern United States are called evergreen rain forests. Tropical rain forests grow in warm places near Earth's equator.

The equator is an imaginary line around the middle of the planet.

Parts of Asia, Africa, Central America, and South America lie along the equator. All of these places have tropical rain forests. The northern tip of Australia has tropical rain forests, too.

About half of all the plant and animal species in the world live in tropical rain forests. There are so many

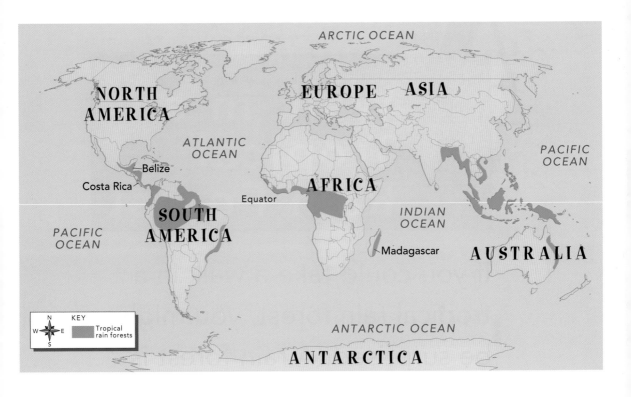

different kinds of plants and animals in the tropical rain forests that no one has counted them all.

A Walk in a Tropical Rain Forest

If you could take a walk in a tropical rain forest, you might be surprised. A rain forest is not filled with animal sounds. It is very quiet. The ground is wet and muddy.

Looking around, you would see huge tree trunks

Many tropical rain forest trees have huge trunks. Smaller plants often grow on the tree trunks.

with small plants growing on them. Looking up, you would see very tall trees

Vines often hang from the branches of rain forest trees.

with vines hanging from their branches. The leaves at the tops of the trees block almost all the sunlight, so it would be very shady on the ground.

Yellow-crowned parrots live in the tropical rain forests of Belize.

High in the trees, you might see some birds. To the right or left, you might see a butterfly. Tiny insects would buzz around you. Many other animals would be hiding above your head and below your feet.

Tropical Rain Forest Animals

The rain forest is full of animals. Frogs and spiders hide under leaves. Snakes slither along the ground and wind around tree trunks.

Ants, beetles, and termites live under tree bark or in the soil. Sloths and anteaters

This eyelash viper (left) lives in the tropical rain forests of Costa Rica. A three-toed sloth (below) spends most of its time in rain forest trees.

hang from tree branches. Wild pigs look for roots under the shady ground.

A spider monkey hangs around rain forest trees all day long.

Many monkeys and other primates live in rain forests. In Central and South America, tiny spider monkeys and white-faced monkeys swing through the treetops. Howler monkeys sit on branches and bark like dogs. Red and green

Ring-tailed lemurs live only on the island of Madagascar.

parrots, black and yellow toucans and many other colorful birds fly through the rain forest.

Huge gorillas roam through the rain forests of Africa. Chimpanzees play in the trees or on the ground. Furry lemurs live only on Madagascar and Comoros, islands near Africa.

Piranhas are fierce fish.

Rain forest rivers are also full of life. Strange fish swim in the muddy waters. A long, skinny fish called the electric eel can stun other animals with an electric shock. Piranhas, fierce little fish with very sharp teeth, usually eat smaller fish. Sometimes they eat larger animals that fall into the water. Piranhas are found in the lakes and rivers of South America's Amazon rain forest, the biggest rain forest in the world.

At night, the rain forest really comes alive. Millions of insects fill the air. Moths suck nectar from flowers. Bats leave their daytime resting places to hunt for insects.

During the day, tent-building bats often rest under the leaves of rain forest trees.

In Central American rain forests, jaguars are at the top of the food chain.

Big wild cats silently stalk the nighttime forest. Jaguars hunt on the ground for wild pigs, rodents, and other animals. Leopards climb through the trees looking for monkeys, birds, and snakes.

Tropical Rain Forest Plants

Many different kinds of plants grow in tropical rain forests. Some are as tall as a 20-story building. Thick parts on their trunks called buttresses keep these trees from falling over.

Special plants called air plants grow on the trunks and branches of many trees. Most

This booyong tree of Australia has impressive buttresses.

plants have roots that take up water and food from the soil, but air plants get water from

These orchids are air plants (left). They grow from the branches of tropical rain forest trees (above).

the air. They get food from the air or from plants rotting nearby. The orchids that grow in rain forests are air plants.

Woody vines called lianas hang from the trees. They also wrap around tree trunks and limbs. Vines called strangler figs can kill trees.

This strangler fig has wrapped itself around a rain forest tree.

The Parts of a Tropical Rain Forest

Why is a tropical rain forest like a birthday cake? Because it has layers. The top layer is called the canopy. It is made of the leaves at the tops of the trees. Many rain forest animals live in the canopy.

A rain forest canopy in Belize

A rain forest understory in Costa Rica (above). An army of ants marches across the rain forest floor in Costa Rica (right).

Below the canopy is a layer called the understory. This layer is made up of tree trunks, young trees, and air plants.

The bottom layer is the forest floor. Few plants grow on the shady forest floor because the soil there is very thin. It is made up mostly of dead parts of plants.

The roots of rain forest trees do not go down very deep, so they can take up only water and food found near the top of the soil.

Why Rain Forests Are Important

Tropical rain forests may seem far away, so you may be surprised to hear that we use many things that come from rain forests. Beautiful woods, such as mahogany, teak, and rosewood, come from rain forest trees.

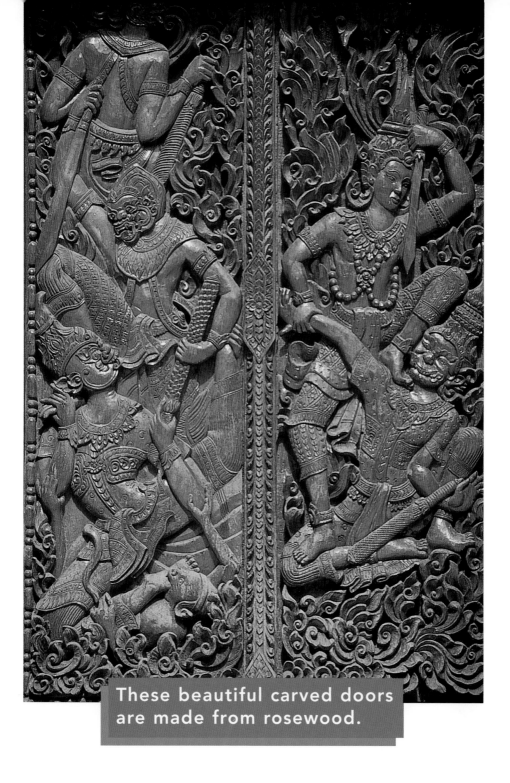

These beautiful carved doors are made from rosewood.

Some of the foods we eat first came from rain forest areas. Bananas were first found in southeastern Asia. Cashews and Brazil nuts come from Central and South America.

Chocolate comes from a bean that grows on the cacao tree. Native peoples found this tree in the Amazon rain forest. They learned to make chocolate from the cacao bean.

Some rain forest plants are also used to make medicines. Quinine, a drug used to treat a disease called malaria, comes

Materials in the leaves of the rosy periwinkle can be used to treat some kinds of cancer.

from the bark of a rain forest tree. A powerful cancer drug comes from the rosy periwinkle that grows in Madagascar.

Scientists think many other rain forest plants could help fight cancer and other diseases.

Rain forests are also important for the environment. People are doing things that may change Earth's climate.

Factories, homes, and cars burn fuel that sends a gas called carbon dioxide into the air. Too much carbon dioxide could trap heat from the sun and make Earth grow warmer. Rain forest trees may help the

Smokestacks on this factory in Michigan send carbon dioxide and other chemicals into the air.

environment by taking large amounts of carbon dioxide out of the air.

Saving Rain Forests

Even though tropical rain forests are so important, they are in danger of being destroyed. Some of the wonderful things that come from rain forests have put the forests in danger.

Too many trees were cut down for their beautiful wood.

At one time, this land was covered with rain forest. Today, it is used for farming.

Rain forest areas were cleared to make room for huge banana plantations. Roads were cut through the forests. Towns and cities were built so that workers would have places to live.

Also, when people in tropical countries need land to grow food or build homes, they clear the rain forest. They cut down all the trees and burn them. Then there are fewer trees to take carbon dioxide out of the air. And burning the trees sends even more carbon dioxide into the air.

Rain forests have been cleared to make room for farming, roads, and buildings.

Harming one plant or animal in a rain forest can harm the whole forest. This is because everything in a rain forest works together. If one living thing disappears, many others may disappear also.

Each of the living things in a rain forest depends on all the others.

Many people are concerned about the environment and want to save rain forests. Some countries with rain forests are trying to help.

Some are buying back the rain forest land that was cleared for farms. But other countries with rain forests say that their people need the land in order to live. This is not an easy problem to solve. Many countries are working to find a way to

save the rain forests and still give people a place to live.

Rain Forest

People have lived in the tropical rain forests of Africa, Asia, and South America for hundreds of years without harming the rain forests. They

This rain forest native is weaving leaves to make the wall for a building.

Peoples

...uild simple houses ...f wood and other ...ain forest plants. ...hey fish and hunt ...or wild pigs and ...onkeys with blow-...uns and darts or ...ows and arrows. ...hey know which ...ain forest plants ...an be used for ...edicines to make them feel ...etter when they are sick.

A native man has caught a large fish in the Amazon River of Brazil.

To Find Out More

Here are some additional resources to help you learn more about tropical rain forests:

 **Books**

Kalman, Bobbie. **Rainforest Birds.** Crabtree Publishing, 1998.

Lewington, Anna and Edward Parker. **People of the Rain Forests.** Raintree Steck-Vaughn, 1998.

Savage, Steven. **Animals of the Rain Forest.** Raintree Steck-Vaughn, 1997.

Silver, Donald M. **Tropical Rain Forest.** McGraw-Hill, 1998.

Woods, Mae. **Plants of the Rain Forest.** ABDO Publishing, 1998.

Organizations and Online Sites

Amazon Interactive

*http://www.geog.umn.edu/
~schaller/amazon/rainforest/
worldmap.html*

Learn all about the Amazon rain forest, the world's largest tropical rain forest.

Animals of the Rainforest Reptile Refuge Society

*http://www.dynaserve.com/
web/reptiles/animals.htm*

Find out about the snakes, frogs, crocodilians, and other animals that live in the world's rain forests.

Kid's Action: Rain Forests Are Full of Life

*http://www.ran.org/ran/
kids_action/life.html*

This site has information about the wildlife and native peoples that live in tropical rain forests

Plants and Animals of Peru's Manu Rain Forest

*http://www.pbs.org/edens/
manu/flora.htm*

Enjoy photos and read interesting facts about a rain forest in Peru.

Welcome to the Tropical Rain Forest

*http://com.simplenet.com/
home.HTML*

Learn about the effort to save the El Choco tropical rain forest on the Pacific Coast of Colombia.

Important Words

air plant a kind of plant with roots that do not grow into the soil

canopy the top layer of the rain forest

carbon dioxide a gas produced when fuel is burned

liana a kind of woody vine

malaria a disease spread by mosquitoes, it can kill people

primates the group of animals that includes chimpanzees, monkeys, gorillas, and humans

soil the dirt and other materials that make up the top layer of Earth

understory the middle layer of the rain forest

Index

Meet the Author

Darlene R. Stille lives in Chicago, Illinois, and is executive editor of the World Book Annuals and World Book's Online Service. She has written many books for Children's Press, including *Extraordinary Women Scientists, Extraordinary Women of Medicine*, four True Books about the human body, and four other True Books about ecosystems.